COCK A DOODLE DOO TO MACBETH

A Collection of Original Poems

Published by Harvey Sagar
ISBN: 978-1-9998573-1-8
www.harveysagar.com

Preface

This book is a collection of original works by the author. Full credit is afforded to the authors of the nursery rhymes, whoever they may be. The originals, prefaced in italics, are followed in each case by the author's interpretation of the possible inner meanings of the rhymes.

The author apologises to Mr. Shakespeare in the recasting of some of his most famous passages. His original writing, again in italics, is followed in each case by the author's borrowing of his style to a modern context, hopefully holding true to his intent.

The remaining poems are completely original but, if there is any resemblance to any existing work, that is entirely coincidental.

Index

Nursery Rhymes

Humour

Life

Shakespeare Revisited

NURSERY RHYMES

Cock a Doodle Doo!

Cock a doodle doo!
My dame has lost her shoe,
My master's lost his fiddlestick,
And knows not what to do.

A cockerel lived on a farm in Cornwall,
Five miles from the road, at the edge of a cliff.
He lived there quite happily alone in his stall
With music, fine wine and the occasional spliff.

The benevolent farmer largely left him alone
But sadly the owner was advancing in years.
One day he felt that the land had outgrown
His ability to cope, even after numerous beers.

He sold the whole lot to a fashionable couple
Who stemmed from a mansion located near Mayfair.
She had fine clothes and a body quite supple;
He always wore ties and an oversized blazer.

He was virtuoso on a fine violin
While she was renowned for just looking good.
She kept her hair tied in a Faberge bobby pin;
His fiddle was made of the finest spruce wood.

In their new home, they loved to wander around
To survey all the land and their new acquisitions.
They would often walk down to the cockerel's ground
Which, to be honest, only served to rouse his suspicions.

A little bit paranoid, he felt them too close;
He disliked her appearance and the man's constant fiddling.
Not only that, the music was morose;
He'd always viewed Shostakovich as middling.

So one day when again they were down near his place,
He decided to sort out the problem for good.
While their emotions ran high with passions apace,
Her clothes and his fiddle lay alone by the wood.

The cock came out rampant as attention was lost
And the bird absconded with all of their chattels.
When the lovers revived, they found to their cost
That the two had lost badly in some unknown battle.

What troubles me most is the loss of my bow
And also my fiddle, said the man. Meanwhile
The fine lady searched around for her shoe,
Feeling angry, disgraced and quite frankly defiled.

The two returned to the house and vowed to never return
But felt lost in their minds as to what they should do.
Meanwhile the victor displayed no concern.
The moral: A cock will just do and do.

Lavender's Blue

Lavender's blue, dilly, dilly, lavender's green.
When I am king, dilly, dilly, you shall be queen.
Who told you so, dilly, dilly, who told you so?
'Twas my own heart, dilly, dilly, that told me so.

Call up your men, dilly, dilly, set them to work,
Some to the plough, dilly, dilly, some to the fork,
Some to make hay, dilly, dilly, some to cut corn,
While you and I, dilly, dilly, keep ourselves warm.

A labourer worked on a farm near to Bude
With girlfriend, a dairy maid, whose first name was Jude.
Their love was so strong it made them act silly,
Like referring to each other with the name, Dilly Dilly.

The man was affectionate and generally kind
But he was arrogant, ambitious and colour blind.
Dreams beyond reason controlled all his thinking;
She shared none of his visions, despite staring and blinking.

One day, she admired the new blossomed lavender
And suggested a photo for the farm's annual calendar.
She said it had the richest blue that she'd seen
But her man said just "No, it was obviously green".

She said, "lavender's blue, Dilly Dilly." but "lavender's green"
Was the riposte of her man, in a manner quite mean.
She asked him from where he had got this idea;
He said that his heart to this conclusion did steer.

He rose to the moment, now fired with emotion,
And decided to share his latest great notion.
He said soon he'd be King and she'd be his Queen,
A future together, the best she'd foreseen.

They could spend all their days in love, rest and talk
And their men on the farm would do all of the work.
She would set some to make hay and some to cut corn,
While they, Dilly Dilly, would keep themselves warm.

Georgie Porgie

Georgie Porgie, Puddin' and Pie,
Kissed the girls and made them cry.
When the boys came out to play,
Georgie Porgie ran away.

George was the second-born son of the Porgies,
Though most people rather called him Georgie.
His two close mates were big fat guys,
Known to all as Pudding and Pie.

The three cruised together, quite badly behaved,
With teenage lust, young women they craved.
They'd scout around the playground at break,
Searching for girls whose love they could take.

But lacking panache, they were really unsubtle
And often dived in for an unwelcome cuddle.
The girls were more streetwise, knew how to resist,
When the boys on their cheek tried to implant a kiss.

Though scarcely bothered, the girls uttered a scream,
Which immediately shattered our teen lovers' dreams.
They'd then augment the young boys' fears
By bursting into uncontrollable tears.

The lads were quite harmless but very inept;
Rejection of their love was hard to accept.
Though the girls clearly showed them utter contempt,
The boys would come back for another attempt.

The girls took a walk round a playing field;
The big hunking footballers had quite an appeal.
But that day there was no trace of the men
Whom they'd previously gazed at, again and again.

Our would-be boy lovers had spied the girls there
And thought they'd persuade them their love to share
But, just as their intention they began to reveal,
Twenty-two strong footballers arrived on the field.

The girls cried out to the men in their kit;
Though not the best looking, they were agile and fit.
When the men waved back, they seemed to be friends
And our boys sensed their romance had come to an end.

When one of the men moved towards the boys three,
Some imminent danger they all could foresee.
The biggest coward could no longer stay
So Georgie Porgie ran away.

Doctor Foster

Doctor Foster went to Gloucester
In a shower of rain.
He stepped in a puddle,
Right up to his middle,
And never went there again.

Doctor Foster was based in Cheltenham
In charge of a GP training programme.
One night, his trainees had all called in sick
So he was on call for the town and the sticks.

About eleven at night, he was lying in bed
With his wife whom he'd just recently wed.
With the ring of the phone, he leapt out of her arms,
Abrupt end to his love, his lust and his charms.

His attention was needed at a suburb of Gloucester
Where someone was suffering with acute herpes zoster.
By the time he set out in his car, a life to maintain,
The weather had changed; it was pouring with rain.

When he arrived at Quedgeley, the rain was still teeming
And he'd lost his temper; in fact, he was steaming.
When he at last found the house, he was tired, soaked and freezing;
Then he found that his patient had gone out for the evening.

In a state of high anger, he went back to his car
And, even though it was parked not that far,
His walk back was hazardous in the depth of the night,
Not helped that the Council had not fixed the lights.

It was not just the lighting that the Council neglected
For the pavement was also left unprotected.
Small potholes left unattended for years
Had now become caverns needing major repairs.

In the dark, our doctor stumbled and fell
Into one of these pits, now full of water as well.
He was drenched from his feet right up to his waist
And smelt strongly of slime and animal waste.

When he got back home and saw his wife there in bed,
All the evening's bad feelings he was able to shed.
He gazed on her with an air expectant
But she told him to bathe in a strong disinfectant.

From that day on, he would no more go to Gloucester;
No more would he kind empathies foster.
If his trainees could not go out to the country,
Neither would he, to speak frankly, quite bluntly.

Goosey Goosey Gander

Goosey Goosey Gander where shall I wander,
Upstairs, downstairs and in my lady's chamber
There I met an old man who wouldn't say his prayers,
I took him by the left leg and threw him down the stairs.

I always used to ask my goose if a problem I did ponder;
People's views were useless and I could cope with them no
longer.
My goose was wise and travelled well, no better friend you'd
pick;
He supervised our house and farm and never missed a trick.

One day, he'd done his usual tour, the rooms, the whole estate.
I asked him where to concentrate, where effort would show
most weight.
He said downstairs, the staff to sort, but not to linger long;
Upstairs is where you need to be for there's a lot that's wrong.

Go to the bedrooms, search around but most the lady's
chamber;
I have to say, though it hurts to do, there's much you will not
savour.
I knew I could trust my beloved mate so took his advice with
haste
And on going through my lady's door, saw sights not to my
taste.

A man of advancing years was there, doing his best to please my girl
But nought was going according to plan; neither seemed in much of a whirl.
He looked despondent, truly sad, so I appealed to the good side of his nature;
Forgiveness would surely come his way, if he managed to pray to his maker.

But he spurned my offer, never finding need of help from a spiritual life
And though, in an accident, had lost his right leg, still felt need of a really good wife.
His cheek was laid bare as he limped to the door, saying my girl must be his betrothed.
A fit of anger in a flash enthralled me and the man I forgave I suddenly loathed.

My goose was not there but seemed to speak and told me what I should do;
This man a lesson had to be taught and I just had to follow it through.
Though he'd only one leg, he was after my wife and I lost all my cares
So I took him by the left leg and threw him down the stairs.

Oh Where, Oh Where Has My Little Dog Gone?

Oh where, oh where has my little dog gone;
Oh where, oh where can he be?
With his ears cut short and his tail cut long,
Oh where, oh where is he?

A lady in Bootle had a sweet little poodle
That she felt could be a winner at Crufts.
She was ready to spend on the kit and caboodle,
If on the outcome she felt she could trust.

She searched yellow pages for the best beauty parlour,
For one that could transform her pet,
With a neatly groomed coat and a diamond collar,
For celebrity in the dog world all set.

She found a salon on Hope Street in Liverpool
And discussed with them all her needs:
Her pet must have ears with long hair, old school,
And a short tail like the best of his breed.

The poodle was sensitive; when he heard of her plans,
At first he felt really worried
But she explained he'd be in the very best hands,
So off to the parlour he scurried.

Sad to relate, the beautician mixed up
The instructions, though clear to the letter.
She imparted short ears and long tail to the pup,
The reverse of what his owner knew better.

When she saw the result, the lady was really upset
And buried her head in her hands.
The dog was more so and started to fret,
Then ran away to some unknown land.

When she uncovered her face, the poor dog had gone;
She searched around low and high.
But the fact he was missing quite quickly did dawn
And at full voice, she started to cry:

Oh where, oh where has my little dog gone;
Oh where, oh where can he be?
With his ears cut short and his tail cut long,
Oh where, oh where is he?

Hark, Hark, The Dogs Do Bark

Hark, hark the dogs do bark;
The beggars are coming to town,
Some in rags and some in jags
And one in a velvet gown.

Mayfair had never been troubled
By beggars at work on the streets;
But recent days had brought new ways
And now they were under your feet.

Mayfair Council had looked at the trend
And decided the guys were in gangs.
They came en masse, parked on the grass,
Sat down and held out their hands.

Vicious dogs they kept as friends
To keep all contenders at bay.
When the dogs barked, the locals marked
Arrival of a new begging day.

Sadly, truly, these folk weren't alone
But paid by a big man in charge.
He lived far away, in a big house did play,
Reaped money from his lackeys at large.

Payment varied on what they had earned,
On what they had fleeced from the crowd.
Some stayed poor while some gained more;
The boss man gave each as allowed.

So it was that when they came
All kinds of richness you'd see.
Some bore scars; others drove cars,
Their clothing mixed smart with carefree.

Fine clothes on some you'd see
While others were totally drab.
Some came in Rolls, others in Scholls,
Some walking, others in cabs.

"Hark, hark, the dogs do bark,"
Said a local when they came into town:
"Some are in rags and one drives a Jag
And one's in a velvet gown."

Pat A Cake

Pat a cake, pat a cake, baker's man,
Bake me a cake as fast as you can.
Prick it and pat it and mark it with "B"
And put it in the oven for baby and me.

Jennifer Robinson lived in a town,
Famous for bakeries, throughout, up and down.
Heavily pregnant, she had not planned for July,
When celebration was expected at the baby's first cry.

Now late in June, her mind belatedly focussed
On some sort of occasion to make the birth noticed.
A grand buffet meal for her family and friends
She decided would satisfy and make amends.

Uncertainty pervaded her mind as to what
Would give greatest pleasure but not cost a lot.
Should she serve paté with toast or extravagant cake?
At this stage of the process, no mistake must she make.

Her final solution was a blend of the two
And find someone who with skill could just see it through.
She scoured the high street, all the bakeries she scanned,
Until she centred on one that looked especially grand.

She appealed to their nature to do everything fast
And hopefully bake something just as she asked.
Like them, she said, she had a bun in the oven,
Whose name would be Billy, just like his cousin.

She said that she needed a cake made of pate,
To be served with coffee, cappuccino or latte.
The cake must be blazoned in the name of her son
And produced with a speed that was second to none.

She said paté cake, paté cake, baker's man,
Bake me a cake as fast as you can.
Prick it and pat it and mark it with "B"
And put it in the oven for baby and me.

Pop Goes the Weasel

Half a pound of tuppenny rice,
Half a pound of treacle;
That's the way the money goes,
Pop! goes the weasel.

Wally Weasel lived in a house,
Near to a London market.
His hobby was to eat too much;
Food was his target.

Market food was terribly cheap
And sold in massive hampers.
Though Wally dragged a lot back home,
First he ate the samples.

Wally's day was spent in a chair,
Eating 'til he floundered.
Exercise was out of bounds
So he grew rounder.

Half a pound of tuppenny rice,
Half a pound of treacle,
Mixed together in a bowl:
Yum! said the weasel.

Wally had no time for work,
Much too busy eating.
Sadly all his money went;
Cash he was needing.

Fatter and fatter grew our friend,
A bursting gut near lethal.
Then he crammed in one more bun;
Pop! went the weasel.

Ding Dong Bell

Ding dong bell,
Pussy's in the well.
Who put her in?
Little Johnny Flynn.
Who pulled her out?
Little Tommy Stout.
What a naughty boy was that
Try to drown poor Pussycat,
Who ne'er did any harm
But killed all the mice
In the Farmer's barn!

It was Sunday and the church bells were ringing;
The choir and congregation were singing.
But, deep in the village well,
For a cat there sounded death knell.

Yes, there while the church was resounding,
A pussy cat was close to drowning.
The perpetrator of this vile crime?
Johnny Flynn, who'd not grown with time.

The boy was short of stature
And stricken with a quite cruel nature.
His father ran the farm
Where the cat had done the mice harm.

Though Kitty had just followed nature,
Young Johnny had quite learned to hate her.
Because he'd made friends with the mice,
Other creatures he'd found much less nice.

He'd fed them with all the best cream
And half the cow's cheese, so it seemed.
But one day the barn was a scene
Of dead bodies, all mice a has-been.

It was thus he sought his revenge
For the life of his friends to avenge.
That's why he headed out to the well
With the cat, all his angers to quell.

The policeman on beat round about
Was called Little Tommy Stout.
Although his real surname was Whittle,
He was nicknamed as fat and belittled.

Tommy was passing by the scene
Where Johnny planned his crime obscene.
He fished out the cat in a jot
And arrested the boy on the spot.

When the case appeared at court,
Tommy had his evidence to report.
The judge then gave a final decision
That treated the boy with derision:

"What a naughty boy was that
Try to drown poor Pussycat,
Who ne'er did any harm
But killed all the mice
In the Farmer's barn!"

HUMOUR

Adam and Eve

When Adam met Eve in the Garden of Eden,
He thought I quite like God's idea of creation:
A fine looking girl, quite the best that I've seen;
Maybe I could be King and she could be Queen.

We've a large, fine estate with very few neighbours
And trees full of fruit with many fine flavours.
We don't need to worry too much about clothes;
Fig leaves will ensure none of our modesty shows.

The one big downside is that snake in the grass,
Who at every turn to my girl makes a pass.
He promises her more than I ever could,
Like a socking great apple and a house in the wood.

I'll tell you one day he'll destroy all our dreams
For Eve is quite gullible, at least so it seems.
I'll bet that eventually she'll succumb to his charm
When all that he offers is nothing but harm.

Well, I'll tell you this, if she gives in to this guy,
And all his false offers she freely does buy,
I'll be leaving this garden and take my girl too
And God knows what on earth we two then will do.

1960s Manchester

I wandered lonely in a cloud;
Sorry, Wordsworth, but that's what I did.
The sixties were great in Manchester,
Apart from the cloying winter smog.

It can't be normal to blow soot from your nose
Or to believe the town hall was built black.
There's a lot to be said for sense of direction
When your far sight is limited to inches.

At least, we could leave the school early
When fog blocked the far side of the quad.
But still the slow buses, the trudge across town
And getting home late though usually alive.

From the bus, great swathes of barren land
Punctuated only by solitary pubs,
Endless supplies of drink for no-one,
Slum clearance, all the people now gone.

Moved to the inner city high rise flats,
Accommodated in cleaner but inelegant buildings,
They gazed out on the beauty of Manchester's skyline,
Distant pubs, more flats and the fog.

Visit to a Show Garden

Two volunteers turned up to the Garden
To assist with the entries and sales from the shop.
It was snowdrop season, no doubt would be busy;
The queues would be long, the work would not stop.

A group of about forty arrived all at once
In a coach that travelled that morning from Dover.
Meals were pre-ordered but the group arrived late
And were told that at two p.m.lunch serving was over.

in a sense, they were lucky for another group that day
Had arrived well on time but to eat had to wait.
The dining room staff said they would give them some food
But, though now one o'clock, they might wait until eight.

The two volunteers set to work on the tills
As usual with one for each person to use.
They were just about coping in reducing the wait
Whilst apologising for delays with profuse excuse.

Then management suddenly appeared on the scene,
Alerted by the workload pressure, some solution to find.
At the end of the day, both tills would be full
And to check out them both, he felt disinclined.

To deal with just one would cut down the load
On the person whose role was to add up the money
So he took one till away, said I'm sure you will manage.
Then made some joke which was not at all funny.

One volunteer now redundant, he went for a coffee
While the other near wept as the queuing got longer.
When complaints grew and grew, the manager came back
Looked at the crowd, stroked his chin and did ponder.

Then he made his pronouncement, in a statesman-like way,
How devoted he was to make it all work:
Next time you come back, he explained to the crowd
Don't come all at once; bring some food and a fork.

The Charity

"Hello," said the caller, "I hope I'm not bothering you
But I'm interested to work with people who care.
I hear that your motives are faithful and true
And your volunteers have insight and flair."

"Is it true that you only take on the best;
That is, those with a feel for the needful,
The people who have utmost willing and zest
And for the poor are constantly heedful?"

"If all that is true," said the lady with feeling,
"And no holds in your endeavours would bar,
Your organisation would be to me most appealing;
With you, I could most certainly go far."

"Thank you for your call," said the girl on the phone,
"We are seeking volunteers who have passion.
I can say that the seeds of your interest are sown
In our field of unstinting compassion."

"In which areas of need would you feel most at home?
We have marriages, unemployment and illness;
There's also the homeless and people who roam
And those who have failed in their business."

"I'm involved with all those," said the caller in tears,
In a tone that was wholesome and credible.
"I know how it's hard to live on cocaine and beers;
Even in Tesco the food seems inedible."

"No doubt we could use you," said the charity's agent.
"Your expertise could make you a member
Of a team here devoted to caring and patience.
Can you start sometime in December?"

"Indeed I could do that but I wish it were earlier.
Any chance we could backdate to September?
My bank's agents have called me and could hardly be surlier
To demand I'm in credit by November."

"I think you'll find benefit in your work with our charity,"
Said the girl in extolling its virtues.
The supplicant was content at this statement of clarity
And that her application would not be refused.

"I'd be pleased with a benefit but I ask you most earnestly
If it could be two, three or four, maybe more.
All the areas you described apply to me perfectly.
You can do bacs, cheque or cash through my door."

Compensation in Law

When a man tripped over the kerb at the mall,
Some people were concerned for his welfare.
He felt more important was to sue for the fall
So he called up a lawyer from a seat on a chair.

Even though he had no injuries to see,
His solicitor advised, and indeed with some stress,
That compensation of thousands he could surely foresee
Were the Court to acknowledge his mental distress.

"I'm certainly shocked," said the man, "to the core,
As everyone here can quite easily see;
In fact, my emotions cannot take too much more.
By the way, are your services totally free?"

"We work on the basis of no win, no fee,"
Said the fawning, young lawyer at the end of the phone.
"Let your feelings, the bad ones, now just run free;
We'll document the mental harm you've been done."

"The opposition will try to raise a defence
In such cases that you've always been mad.
Can you assure me you've always seen sense
And there's no mental illness that you've ever had?"

The man told him of schizophrenia and shell-shock,
Agoraphobia, mania and a great fear of clowns,
Compensation neurosis and severe writer's block
But no other which he need to note down.

"That is," said the man, "apart from depression,
Obsessive-compulsion and a dislike of crowds,
Social revulsion, unfettered aggression
And going through life with my head in the clouds."

"I don't see a problem," said the lawyer sincerely;
"I know a psychiatrist who'll declare your good health.
I can tell that the accident's affected you dearly.
Don't worry; very soon we will add to your wealth."

New Zealand Holiday

Go hols in New Zealand?
Yes, swim, if you're feelin'.
If it's wine you've got longing on,
Just take on the sauvignon.

You might prefer cities;
Well, Auckland's got pretties.
If hot water will seize yer,
Rotorua has geysers.

Excitement's your bling?
Then Queenstown's the thing.
You've got skydive and bungee
To make your brain spongey.

Don't let the ice pass yer;
Take the car to a glacier.
St Josef's one name
Though it's cold just the same.

You want to see islands?
Then this land is your land.
It's got nearly the most
And they're all near the coast.

Don't miss on the Maoris
Though they're not near the townies.
They've got it all sorted,
An old life that's unthwarted.

There are green and blue lakes,
Steak, seafood and cakes
And high mountains with snow.
Yes, you've just got to go!

Ladies at Leisure

Forty fine ladies all dressed in green satin
Went down to the town's local swimming pool.
Most had their heads bare but one had a top hat on;
She taught posture at a girl's nearby finishing school.

At the turnstile, the attendant said that the lockers were small
And was concerned about the size of their dresses.
He said it unlikely that they'd fit in at all,
Whilst gazing lasciviously at their tresses.

"Don't worry," said the bespectacled lady up front
As she claimed to be a nobleman's daughter.
"In Oxford, our clothing was fine for a punt
And it kept us all warm in the water."

"We all have bus passes," said a dame at the back,
"But how to use them we are quite unsure.
We have heard that some cards can give you cash back
And such services we're keen to procure."

"A bus pass is a pass for the bus," said the man,
"Whilst down here they carry no virtue.
You may as well throw them in our trash can.
I'm sorry - I don't want to hurt you."

"My chauffeur suggested," said a lady in grey,
"To enquire of the pool's current usage.
We would, if required, a large amount pay
To avoid all the proletariat's sewage."

"Stay down at the deep end," said the man with concern,
"You'll find incontinent kids at the other.
And those of your class I sense will discern
Not to mix with young brats and their mothers."

"I'm feeling confused," said a lady in pearls,
"With just one pool end our team would be solo.
But the other must take another team of girls
To complete a real game of polo."

"We have never tried water polo before
But we are all keen to give it a try.
For your advice we would all most keenly implore
And, with practice, would learn by and by."

The man said nothing but the silence was broken
By a loud voice from the back of the cronies.
"Of the polo, one matter has not yet been spoken:
Through which door do we bring in the ponies?"

Modern Art

The picture was a mixture of circles and lines
In bold, garish colours mixed with grass, card and twine.
Two acorns were stuck to the left in a corner;
Small photos of corpses made a macabre border.

Drips of what seemed like fresh blood in the middle
Were framed by small models of a flute and a fiddle.
Something like dung formed a small pile to the right
While, at the far left, was a chunk of egg white.

No-one could surely say that the creation was pretty
Or demanding, intriguing, emotive or witty.
I gazed in bemusement for what seemed a long hour,
While searching for meaning, its content did scour.

A few minutes later, I saw the text analytic,
Written by some incisive, world famous art critic.
I read it quite carefully, then went back to the picture
To search out within its meaningful structure.

The critic explained how the work clearly displayed
How by life's experience one's character is made.
You can see, he explained, the prime role of the mother
And negative feelings that creation can smother.

Most obvious of all was the role of the father,
Most clearly shown by those seeds in the corner.
The ingredients in toto were what made it great
For they clearly combined a strong message to state.

Duly informed, I felt I had to move on
To the next picture called Fresh Flowers Are Gone.
It showed a lot of young cattle at work in a mine;
Sadly, the text of the critic I had to decline.

The New Forms of Art

I'd like to say I enjoy bouncing around
To the rhythm, or not, of yet another boy band,
Discovered on X Factor, though not by the judges,
But by popular vote, the views of the average.

Some C class musicians, who came last on the day
But, from voicemails, texts and all of the techno,
By the people out there were escorted to stardom,
Adored by those who do not like music.

And then we have rap, an exciting new genre,
At least for those for whom opera is boring.
The attraction there is the complete lack of melody,
A new type of verse, a form of bad poetry.

I've examined art in a variety of galleries
And eclectic taste I believe that I have.
Some modern creations are truly exciting,
Whilst others exist just to snub to the past.

But, at least, we have the virtue of critics
Who willingly analyse the pictures we see.
A blank sheet of red apparently shows
The adolescent turmoil of young girls made free.

And poetry's the same; some modern creators
Will write the first thing that comes to their head.
They write a poem, facile and pointless,
Like me, who looks for support from the mindless.

Tomorrow's Adventure

So tomorrow I go under the knife
No feeling, no emotion, no memory
Or so I am told
My soul in the hands of a man
Or two, with nurses and others
Around to give help

I've not studied their qualifications
Nor quizzed them on surgical skills
I just take it all
But they surely seem to be confident
And they certainly know how to talk
Isn't trust wonderful?

Well, I guess we'll see if they're right
When the anaesthetic has finally abated
Assuming I wake
But, if I don't, at least I'll have left
No feeling, no emotion, no memory
Winner both ways

The Cyclist

I was driving down the road when I came across a fly,
Riding on a bicycle, its legs were lifting high.
At least, a fly is what it looked like; its shell was multicoloured
And wrapped around its body so much it seemed quite
smothered.

It's eyes were big and black and covered half its face;
Like all the insects I've ever seen, its expression showed no
trace.
Determined to get on with life, it drove along with purpose,
Appearing unconcerned for things around it and not the least
bit nervous.

Another fly, much like the first, drove close behind the other.
He looked and behaved so similarly he could have been his
brother.
They did not seem to be racing, but sometimes he drew
beside,
Blocking the whole road so no-one could pass them if they
tried.

The road was long and narrow with lots of bends and twists
So my position stuck behind them for miles it did persist.
At last the road was straighter and I thought I'd overtake;
Even though one lurched out sideways, I thought I'd make a
break.

As I passed, the front fly glared, his demeanour clearly ruffled.
He moved with purpose out towards me so to pass I really struggled.
He gave a sign with outstretched fingers to show that he'd been snubbed,
A sun-glassed man in Lycra emblazoned Veterans Cycling Club.

The Vicar

One day, a vicar knelt down in earnest to pray
To spend the next week or maybe two as a cat.
He explained to God that what he did every day
Was just chatting about this and that.

Though congregations on Sundays followed a service devoted
To worship to God and all of His flock,
Every week there was one who was drunken and bloated
And others who just looked at the clock.

With the hymns, the organist was loose on the foot
So the tone could often be misplaced or lacking.
The choir leader tapped out the beat on his boot
And the singers en masse needed sacking.

Admittedly, as a group, the choirboys looked gorgeous
But these days such thoughts are considered improper.
Our friends, Roman Catholics, were somewhat incautious;
Their antics soon brought in the coppers.

The ladies in charge of the flowers quite clearly meant well
But the colours were bold and, quite frankly, clashing.
Unlike their drab dresses with a strong violet smell
Save one lady, whose couture was dashing.

Even the weddings could bring disappointment
When none of the guests had a clue how to pray.
Mothers smelt of cheap scent and grandmas of ointment
And none of the brides would obey.

As a cat, I could explore my surrounds with impunity;
In disguise, I would root out the sins and the squalor.
I could make meaningful change in our community,
Provided nobody spots my dog collar.

The Chiropractor

She ushered me in with a smile and a wave,
Then took all my details while I sat in a chair.
As best as I could, all my symptoms I gave;
Then she said get undressed to be practically bare.

As I lay on her couch wearing just underwear,
I explained that the problem involved only my wrist.
She said that the problem could be anywhere
So she'd need to see all; at least that's the gist.

I knew about the codes for treaters and patients
And how equal roles she should strive to display.
So I asked, without trying to be over-blatant,
Why she was not dressed in a similar way.

To my great surprise, she ignored my request
And started deep massage on all of my joints.
She twisted my back, pressed my shoulders and chest,
Then stuck needles in what she called trigger points.

I have to admit I was really surprised
When she rotated my ankle and hard pressure put on;
I took a deep breath and then opened my eyes
And at once the pain in my wrist had all gone.

Back with my clothes on and feeling pain-free,
I felt my problem would get no second look.
It stayed that way until she told me her fee
And I reached out with anguish to get my cheque book.

LIFE

A Walk Through Life

Trees taller than me
        So frightening
Sun's halos round ash leaves
        So blinding
But the bluebells were pretty

Next I was bigger and the trees got smaller
        Much better
Rabbits and deer and sparrowhawks and owls
        So clever
And the bluebells were pretty

Then I looked down and the children were smaller
        So cute
Heels skipped on gold barley, laughs in the wind
        So happy
And, like the bluebells, so pretty

Now smaller, trees taller
        So slow
Colours dimmer and blurry
        Thoughts blown
But the bluebells were pretty
        Now gone

The Weary Traveller

When earthly space is filled with void
And life stands on the edge of darkness,
When rainbow's colours turn to grey
And melody fades to monotone,

The shimmering rivers lose their glint
And the rush of waves stays static;
Cloud-touching mountains turn to tiny
And birdsong distant memory.

Like beetles, we crawl through the mire;
At day's dawn, we hide from the light.
Our bequest to those who come after
Is cold bones entombed in dark earth.

But carboned corpses feed the earth
And spirits roam the houses;
Brain cells nurture memories;
You cannot get rid of yourself.

Let me ride on the track at the edge of the woods
And make footprints in sea-sodden sand.
Let raindrops drip down my forehead
And, yes, let me also feel pain.

Music will fill my ears when I'm deaf,
Kaleidoscopes bless my blind eyes.
Dispatch my mind from creation;
It goes on ere I wished it not so.

Do We Not All Choose

Do we not all sometimes choose the darkness
When lights of civilisation betray us?
Constraints of order may tax us
But escape has no mercy.

Waves beat the sands which complain not;
Clouds move where the winds may take them;
Winners may rise from trials of conflict
But last they will not.

Shadows provide cover from visions of reality
Yet harbour that which dwells on the lost.
Open space seems free field for ambition
But will temper success.

Do we not all plan for the future
And drain emotion for goals that are lost?
Yet the sands will still rest when we're beaten
And the clouds will keep place in the sky.

Make Light of Your Charms

Make light of your charms for the darkness will deepen you;
Stay bright to the present when the future's unknown.
Today, tonight, are the past come tomorrow;
The future's no more when all's gone before.

In the quietness of solitude, we are blessed with ourselves:
No noise, no intrusion, no worries, no people,
No ventures, no plans, no new looks forward,
No creation, no nadirs, no zeniths - no people.

Sunlight shines not in the depths of the valleys;
From a low point, the vista is upwards to hills.
The cairn at the top gazes down at your baseness
And yet still, far beyond, can confront the new lands.

Children laugh, not for the past or what may yet befall,
The trinkets, the toys, the pleasure of being
Is all. We who latch on and join in the present
Become fully grown children of the new future.

Play Light

Play light with the wind for its whorls will deepen you;
Nature's eyes fast view your imprudence.
Tread softly, no deep impressions to make;
Dark shadows don't hide you.

Trip night's cotton clouds, the starlight in your hair;
Beware day's sun may bleach out your soul.
Take free soft water from the high mountain streams;
Valley's deep rivers may drown you.

Dance on the stones, step with care on the fields;
Take colours from abstract, shun greyness of being.
In life's music of discord, rest in the rhythm;
The melody won't shield you.

Play light in the storms for the blizzards will still you;
Take heed of creation's infidelity.
Stand loose in the waves; lie firm on the sand;
Hold fast to the moment of living.

Shake Off The Scales

Take no part in the riots of sadness
    The bullies there
     will find you and hurt you
They are there
    in the shadows
And can find a soul
     in the gutter

Crawl through the drains
     of misery
If the smell is appealing but I bet
     that it's not
Unless you've shut your mind
     and senses
     to reason

You could break out and fly
     on the clouds
You could live
     on the shoulders
     of people
You could flush out the drains
     and disperse the riots
     float free
And shake off the scales

Show Caution

Take no heed of the lights of promise
When shone with empty deliverance.
Fortune-makers harbour trained credibility,
Camouflaged vipers in a field of the vulnerable.

Is honesty enshrined in a face of openness?
And do the dirty homeless have no virtue?
Light is bent when it passes a prism,
Truth's distorted when passed through the mind.

Uncertainty's the most reliable certainty,
Pure truth is the most likely impure.
Judgement of others is tainted by failure,
Failure of an intellect less precise than it thinks.

Some will prey on that weakness of thought;
Others will translate own inadequacy as kindness.
But decisions made certain today, come tomorrow
May not turn out as our minds thought they'd be.

The Tunnel

Into the tunnel with trepidation I venture,
An inverted cone of restricting freedom.
The chains of life fall on, not off,
Just closure.

Long will be the downhill trajectory,
The infinite in cruel reality portrayed;
A new day's dawn, a new year sung,
Revolving objects.

A job, some money, a bit more food;
Some days with sunshine, most with rain;
Children light within the darkness
Until they're gone.

One more time I'll speak to the sky
And take it deep to my soul.
No doubt I'll see the heaven's rays,
Then clouds.

One day I'll reach the end of the tunnel,
Walls then constrained on body and soul,
Choices absent, an impassable block,
The end.

Stay and Go On

Into the swamp of glorious delusion
Swim your ambitions, projects and hopes.
The life of the mire eat up the unready,
When predators you allow them to be.

The new in is out;
Forward the new backward;
Lounge in the present,
Future without you.

The stripes of beating have colours,
The pain of trauma a feeling.
Deafness hears no bad noises
And no harmonies.

The life of life is life itself;
The death of life is absence.
Control of infinity is love of the finite;
Stay with it and go on.

Contrasts

With every dawn rise, a twilight will follow;
When sun shines, sometime rain will come.
The joy of child's birth heralds some adult's sad death
And still we hope for the future.

Love's joy is matched by its grieving;
Found love is matched by its loss.
The humour that leads us to laugh
Is so often at someone's expense.

The colours of spring flowers all die away,
Whole beauty, such potential all lost.
The cry of a baby, a route to its speaking;
The cry of an adult, its sole mode of needing.

Yet comes on the autumn, warm colours, cool air,
The knell of a lifehood, some lost and some gained.
And cold harshness of winter, the slips on the ice,
But fields of snow powder reflect golden light.

The Young Vision

Once I was young in a world of balance:
The stars revolved around me and my life;
New love, true love, for ever,
The future determined from then.

But then random kicks in, you learn about chaos,
How reason sometimes hides its face.
Small things become big, illogical logical,
And conviction is subsumed in the transient.

A life of meandering pathways we meet.
We're presented, at each turn, with such choices
But not ones removed from unforeseen influence,
Just direction amongst Brownian motion.

Is experience really an honest teacher?
And, if so, just exactly what does it teach?
To look for reason in irrationality? Impossible,
Or to hark back to when we were blind to those things?

Rise and Fall

Keep the troubles out of your kitbag;
Don't fling out the tools at your anguish.
Sharp chisels will cut and blunt hammers
Give blows. But reason will conquer.

Flat-sheeted fields have no mountains
But also no views. A fast route
From the seabed is up to the surface,
Though waves will still crest and tumble.

The spectrum kaleidoscopes colours
But the brightest of lights can blind.
Noises can harmonise music
But the loudest can shut out your ears.

Take heed of extremes and wed with
The moderate. The perfect evades us
The more in pursuit of its goal
Until high rise flows fast into deep sink.

Live on high lows, take base as the centre;
Hard blows are the softest when the worst are
Made known. The tools that bear injury are
The ones that also create.

A Winter's Tale

When frozen crystals gather on shimmering pavements
And wintry sun shines light of false hope,
A man in wet rags takes off to his bedroom
By the recycling bins of a supermarket chain.

Within walls of damp cardboard, the dormitory's settled;
Three or four men all friends, and the rats,
Seek a night of escape from another day of survival
In the hope that the dawn will herald new life.

But abuse and intolerance, their meat for the day,
Mixed perhaps with dessert of some love and compassion,
Await their wakening thoughts of each day,
Subdued by one greater, that the sleep just continues.

Get a job's good advice, if one were on offer.
Stop the drugs quite good too, if only I could.
Stop the drinking and spend your money on food.
Yes, fine, but how else to escape from earth's torment?

Did I ask to see a friend blown up by a bomb?
Have a wife whose love lived in butterfly's wings?
Was I blessed when I was plagued by none of those things
But turned out to be what people like to call useless?

So bring on world's freeze, knife-like winds, beds of ice,
Blistered toes, cramping pains and icicled digits,
Inner fire lost of fuel, embers lying now cold,
All nurtured by cold hearts of those who pass by.

Surgical Spirit

Patient asleep, the skin now opened,
Deeper tissues now all exposed.
A red, warm blanket of life beneath,
The surgeon's bed to explore.

Confidence takes him into the known;
Anxiety fears the unknown.
How many times had he treated the cause
And in how many was he proved wrong?

The wife had cried when he told her the news,
The scalpel to violate his body.
Endearings that all would be for the best
Just caused her to shed yet more tears.

Now bodily parts once sacred to him
Are exposed and gain public view.
Humiliation and treatment, all wrapped into one:
That's medicine; that's what we must do.

And supposing it's worse and he dies on the table,
Our plans to change life all gone wrong?
Who will explain that it's fate that has done it
And that's what we never can change?

Well, it's down to him, the surgeon, the violator,
The one who gave hopes now destroyed.
But, in that moment, not just one life is lost
But many more who will dwell in his grievance.

Pride

Misgivings, the lot of those with conscience,
Denial, the blanket of awareness,
Compete in the ring of ego's battle,
Where I am me and me is all.

Tomorrow, where yesterday is gone,
Becomes this day revisited,
When experience chooses hiding
And tomorrow becomes today.

Far from the darkness of days past,
Horizon's sun lights roads to plenty
Through astigmatic eyes of sultry vision,
Where learning teaches nothing.

When all is gone, stand proud in empty;
Make firm of quicksand 'neath your feet;
And cherish in the joy of absence,
'Til death confirms the role you seek.

Feel the Edge

Fortunes of unknown, wonders of uncertainty,
The gaps in a starlit sky;
The walk through an overgrown forest,
Roots we do not perceive.

The seen, the unseen and then the seen different,
Perception guided by conscience,
Mould the reality of life's blank canvas;
A picture is what you create.

Stand on the branches of instability
As birds do with measure.
Plough through the earth of resistance
Into darkness, happy, like moles.

Or fry on a heat-baked lounger, blinded
By the sun that you seek.
One day, your god will come back to visit
In a malignant backlash.

Night is dark only because day is light;
The stars don't fall, just hide;
Light glistens in colours on crystals of ice
Only because it is cold.

Stand on the edge and look down at the fall
Or ponder, feel pride at your height.
The opposites all have opposites themselves;
It's one end or the other.

Field of Dreams

Build steel covers over the heart of anguish;
Put resilient plugs in the well of despair.
Then lie with ease in a field of dreams
That won't come true.

This day heralds future; have no past in today.
Infinity's finite when imagines have gone.
Seats of hard rock become cushions of comfort
When you let them.

Put the steel covers under the seat of forward
And plugs in the drains of your love;
Then take ease in a field of dreams
That will come true.

Hand in Hand

I'd like to see the mountains shake
And the wind go deathly quiet,
The earth stand still, the sun go dark
And roses lose their colour.

I'd like to see the rain go upwards
And, when snow falls, feel warm,
The lava going back to craters
And fish walking from the sea.

I'd like to see my love in scarlet,
Fine lace and jewelled fingers,
Dressed hair in ringlets, flowing gold,
Nature's beauty rightful shown.

I'd like to sense her warming heart
When my hand holds hers in mine,
To know that love will be returned
When my soul to her I offer.

I'd like to see the world with me
And her, we both, just us.
I'd like to see a lot of things
Yet more believe they'll happen.

Absence

In the depths of your clouds, no silver lining;
On blinkering sunlight, the shutters put down.
Crescendos of opera now repeated discord;
Scales of bad notes play random melody.

Come call to the conductor of life's accord,
In chaos of random some synthesis foreseen
To still out the bounces and flatten the contours
That blunt your intentions at every day's morn.

In your quagmire, there still shines the sparkle
That glints through those gaps you don't see.
But thunderclouds crowd o'er the hope of insight
To block you from life and from me.

The end is too clear, a plain sheet of blackness:
No images, no colours, no motion, no sense.
The light is turned off, the soundbox is silent
And all that I'm left with is absence.

Just You

There was a time when I thought I knew you.
How wrong could I be, how troubled?
Your fawning face, your eyes of depth,
Your soul that lacked fulfilment.

A depth of nonsense, a veneer of gilt,
Affection bounded by rules;
A love that stretched beside itself
To view yourself from beyond.

You found no place in a world of fact
Nor solace in the sheets of emotion.
Your focus was centred on love,
Especially when directed to you.

Bad things happen, it's always been so;
Don't blame your friends for disaster.
Why do you just want to protect yourself
In a world that's desperately needy?

OK, go forward, and stand firm to the winds;
Make sure you do not go under.
But I'll tell you, if you continue to go on your own,
You may find that you're always alone.

You and True Love

You said that you loved me but I know that you didn't;
Your promises were all weasel words.
When you said it was me who would share in your future,
I recognise now, just a front.

You were the loveliest thing that I'd ever seen;
Your eyes seemed to shine in the darkness.
A face with expressions like those of an angel,
A laugh of sublime melody.

Sometimes we give our whole selves unconditionally;
What a mistake that turned out to be.
For me, devoting myself to a traitor,
A traitor to love and to me.

The money doesn't matter, the flowers and the jewels,
Given gladly to one I adored.
But to be faithless in spirit and deny honesty;
Well, now I wish that we'd never met.

One day, the clouds will break in the sky;
God's gift will be by my side,
Someone who can give what I'd give to them.
Until then, let us just say goodbye.

One Mother and Her Child

From the distance, a proud figure strutting:
Female form, sullen pout and eyes on fire,
Closer now and bigger yet:
An overpowering matriarch.

Behind, a girl in tatters, slow and stumbling,
A face of porcelain purity, eyes of innocence,
Barely keeping up the triggered pace
And failing targets yet again.

A front stage of dominance and a shadow of submission
Walk in train in hierarchical procession;
Two souls defined by the mind of the single;
Duality of person forced merged into one.

Love of motherhood as a virtue of firm discipline
Grounds the child's future as a mirror of her own;
Maybe strengthens the soul that weakens;
Maybe subsumes the one that's vulnerable.

Ambition for a daughter, perhaps an ego transferred,
But still creation blesses free spirit.
Dull buds will blossom to mature florescence
When the weeds don't stifle their glory.

Manchester Terrorism May 2017

Limbs thrown as garbage
Against the kiosks
And people;
Walkways now blood puddles,
Concentrated by hatred
And diluted by tears.

Explosions: then people ran
But to nowhere
And everywhere
At once.
Where to find safety?
And reason?

The homeless and privileged
Joined in a vice of emotion
And aid;
And the concert came back,
The concert of music
And defiance.

In the name of love,
Of God, the terror was done:
An attempted blight of humanity
That suffered
And love
That survived.

So, not well done, you outside men,
Gains are judged by its losses.
Evil that gains
On the day
Faces love of humanity
That rests eternal.

Once I Trod

Once I trod on my daughter's toes,
An accident hurting me more than her.
Then later my foot crushed wild flowers,
Her beneath my feet.

When she struggled to pull field grasses
And stumbled on gravel outgrowth,
Bruised and crying, yet still admonished
Saw mischief, hurt and blame entwined.

A laughing, free streak that spread to the world
But, hampered by society's controls,
No more could she let out her full spirit
An artist constrained by the rules.

Yet now she's released to laugh in the wind
To create colour in infinity's blackness,
To make harmony amongst the random notes
And feel free from humanity's binds.

But, if feet had never trampled on virtue
Or suppressed expansion of mind,
Just let the one what she wanted to do,
Would the world have gained or have lost?

The Dearest Has Gone

When your dearest departs this earth
The world stops spinning
Except it doesn't
It all carries on going round
Unchanged, unyielding
Yet something missing

Memories harbour hurt, so kindless
I wish they were gone
For now and ever
But they come back uncalled, unwanted
Unchanged, unyielding
For one missing

Next day's the day after today
One more follows that
And so it goes on
New ventures all old, new comforts
All cold, the warmth
Now totally absent

In the morning, light shines on your earth
To tease your existence
Somehow to reality
But it fails when the clouds hide the sun
And cut out the vibrance
At least in your mind

When I Cast My Eyes

When I first cast my eyes on your face,
You were deep in a world of dreams.
So peaceful, so tranquil, so lovely;
For ever it would be, so it seemed.

When I first saw you running through fields,
The barley rising over your waist,
The sun shimmered on your golden hair,
A child so pure and so chaste.

When I saw you smile, I laughed;
When I saw your tears, I wept;
When I saw you stumble, I fell;
Such beauty, so normal, so perfect.

I tried to be by your side,
Closer than me to myself,
To point you to joy and fulfilment,
To a life of spiritual wealth.

Your existence itself gave me life;
In your growth, I grew also with you;
Your pleasures made me so happy;
We had a bond so firm and so true.

In your sickness, I shared in your ills;
As you worsened, my life too declined.
When you left, a part of me vanished,
Our potential for ever denied.

When I now cast my eyes on your face,
You still seem lost in your dreams.
So peaceful, so tranquil, so lovely;
No more can it be, so it seems.

Whoever Devised Regrets?

Whoever devised regrets?
Chained in withdrawal;
Anchored self-pity;
Closed doors at the dusk, no more dawn.

Whoever implanted bad memories?
Lost pages revised;
Books blocked in mid-read;
New chapters written for no-one.

Whoever invented the past?
Bad histories retained;
Virtues now gone;
A battle with what may yet happen.

Whoever thought of depression?
Pictures of sorrow;
More black paint than gold;
Maybe He who first thought of regrets.

Lost Love

Glistening raindrops track clear glass panes,
Liquid diamonds in an ambient sun.
Teardrops stream on satin skin,
Ambushed emotion placed on view.

Close bonds that fired the blinding light,
The world to take eternal shadow,
Now broken as the miller's wheel,
With stone its substitute for grain.

Far gone, creation's budding spirit;
Too soon lost, the seeds of life;
A long decline to depths of hell;
The future, that awaits me now.

Let light no longer shine on raindrops
And flatness smooth the earth's contours.
When this weary trial is over,
Sun and hills may rise again.

Return, lost love, to your resting place,
Strange bodies merged as one,
Where space and time become subsumed
In just we two, new citadel.

Pictures and Dreams

When I saw you on the wall of my bedroom,
I saw a portrait in pastels and oils,
The colours so vibrant, the contours so rounded,
A portrait of perfection made real.

But real it was not because you had gone
And all that was left was an image.
But the image then faded, the pastels and lines
Dissolved to a quagmire of grey.

How cruel is the night, how real seem the dreams
A life in a world far from here
Until here comes back and the hope fades away
To give space to a land dark and flat.

Bring back my picture, leave me lost in my dreams,
Take away the hurt of reality
Unless just one day you'll maybe come back,
Then no need of the pretence and icons.

Dreams

Have you ever wondered how dreams work?
Where roads of life take random paths
And love, hate, envy merge as one
Or dissipate without direction.

The place where past will follow future
And unreason now takes reason.
Memories of real past distorted,
The bad to good and good to awful.

Solutions to problems, all logic denied,
And stories no author has so far written.
Images brighter than colourful canvas
Coalesce in a few moments glory.

Past enemies and friends become united,
Old lovers, now current, all taken as one.
The things that you wished you had done before
Are now finished with an end unexpected.

Oh, to live in that half-lost life,
Much more thrilling than the one that we have.
No questions asked; that's just how it is
And surprise appears at every corner.

The Pianist

Fingers like humming birds hovered on treble keys,
A trill seeking nectar from flowers of the harmony;
The left hand, a friend, in concert of rhythm,
Two hands, an extension of brain and of art.

There he sits, creator and seeker,
Expression transfixed, in the world of horizon
Moving the earthly to a new sphere, ethereal,
Limbs movements, once concrete, now abstract.

Birds fly in melody, ants crawl through pathos;
We despair in discord and take rest in cadence,
The world a symphony, cantata, sonata;
Beauty built from its meaningless fragments.

Can love live in piano keys?
Are human souls constructed from music?
When flesh's gone, and bare souls are left,
Is eternal the art that remains?

The Hills of Scotland

I danced solo Gay Gordons over bracken's heath
And heard pibrochs in the curlew's cry.
Rabbits ran soft; the thunder came hard;
Capercaillies kept their distance.

From far away, the skylark's aria
Rang through the threatening of waves.
The cliffs beheld their moody presence;
The peregrines sat biding their time.

Razored rain cut through my skin
As harebells upheld their dignity.
The horizon came closer with each passing gale
Until universe swept over my shoulder.

Winds closed my eyes and shut out my hearing
To leave me drifting in the blanket of quiet;
Bright sky's rays winked through gaps in the darkness,
A lantern slideshow in a blackened room.

The hail, the sun, the rain and flowers
Merged in one kaleidoscopic sense;
A tableau of love in a sea of emotion
That grounded me in our Scotland's hills.

The Mountains

The sun bade goodnight behind the peaks
Leaving pink kisses on shining white patches;
Away for the night. Granite peaks now alone
Stand with still respect and majesty.

Sun's fresh kiss in the dawn, a bright yellow one,
Unites the two friends for the start of new day.
Cotton clouds bless their welcome reunion
And rain showers refresh love's thirst.

They may separate and stand alone for each night
But tomorrow will be there; and the next
And the next and the next; and the next forever
When we lie inert beneath their feet.

When we can translate that harmony of being
To ourselves as visitors in their land,
Only then may we rise to the level of grandeur
That nature provides as the final example.

It holds no pride and harbours no grudges
Like we who battle to gain but destroy.
So cherish sun's kisses on hills' welcoming lips,
Saying goodnight, I will be there in the morning.

The Pink Lake

I stumbled round sand dunes, under eucalyptus branches,
To a sheet of iridescent pink,
A sea of bubble-gum liquid with slight, shallow ripples:
Blancmange with a wedding-cake icing.

A bird became my friend while staring from a branch,
A coat of deep blue, a balaclava of green,
A bright nose ring of crimson and a collar of white;
Welcome to my home, said his eyes.

Say hello to my orchids: blue, tiny, silky and shy
And over there's yellow; don't leave him out.
The Banksias, our farmers, feed the birds, bats and bees
And maybe you too, if you settle in here.

The ringneck was persuasive and I could not ignore him.
I could share bed room with plovers, if willing,
Or his mates, banded stilts, may find space in their nests,
Though take care of silver gulls from above.

So had I now found heaven? Had I died without knowing?
The harmony and grace were ethereal.
With the sound of the birds in my ears, I gazed back at the
lake;
Pink final colour of peace.

The Rose Garden

The man at Chelsea had planted roses
No gardenias, hollyhocks, dahlias or foliage
Just roses
Deep red, pale red, bright pink and blue
Tall ones, small ones, thin ones, fat ones
All roses

Others constructed posies but he just grew roses
No decoration, stonework, garlands or statues
Just roses
The judges praised the vast sea of colour
The symmetry, perspective, inspiration and depth
Created by roses

Bronze medal, silver medal, perhaps even gold
Might await a creator of such original art
Produced by roses
And, yes, he succeeded, top award he was granted
In acceptance, key players in his venture he cited
The roses

No one in particular, they all played a role
Each flower was unique but together an ensemble
Of roses
Created a whole much greater together
Than when each flower was displayed on its own
A rose garden

SHAKESPEARE REVISITED

The Tempest Act IV Scene 1

You do look, my son, in a moved sort,
As if you were dismay'd: be cheerful, sir.
Our revels now are ended. These our actors,
As I foretold you, were all spirits and
Are melted into air, into thin air:
And, like the baseless fabric of this vision,
The cloud-capp'd towers, the gorgeous palaces,
The solemn temples, the great globe itself,
Ye all which it inherit, shall dissolve
And, like this insubstantial pageant faded,
Leave not a rack behind. We are such stuff
As dreams are made on, and our little life
Is rounded with a sleep. Sir, I am vex'd;
Bear with my weakness; my, brain is troubled:
Be not disturb'd with my infirmity:
If you be pleased, retire into my cell
And there repose: a turn or two I'll walk,
To still my beating mind.

The Well-Dressed Beau

Your new look, my son, may be a groovy sport
But, if you've mirth displayed, be fearful, sir;
The devil's prowls are endless. There are factors
Fast behold you, worth prohibits and
Art shelters in despair, of which beware.
And mind the tasteless fabric of the season:
The proud capped collars, the taught embraces
Of blossomed stencils to strait enrobe oneself.
See all which it dismerits shall resolve
Fast rise to cry this fragile fashion dated.
Leave all the racks behind. Don't wear such stuff
Where jeans have quilt on, and some brittle knife
Has founded fissures deep. Sir, I'm perplexed;
Wear not in cheapness; arraign in buckles;
Be not absorbed with diversity.
If you'd me please, attire upon thyself
The fairest clothes. Concern for you, I'll talk,
Until your breeding's found.

Hamlet Act III Scene 1

To be or not to be, that is the question
Whether it's nobler in the mind to suffer
The slings and arrows of outrageous fortune
Or to take arms against a sea of troubles
And, by opposing, end them. To die - to sleep
No more; and by a sleep to say we end
The heartache, and the thousand natural shocks
That flesh is heir to - it's a consummation
Devoutly to be wish'd. To die, to sleep -
To sleep, perchance to dream. Ay, there's the rub

Dietary Advice

To eat or not to eat? Bad indigestion,
Together with broken inner wind, to suffer
The things that harbour contagion's fortune
To make harm against one's steel and muscle
And, by their poisoning, send them to die. Or to weep
No more, to keep at bay and not pretend
That part-baked cows and cloudy mackerel stock
Refreshly bear you. 'Tis a consumption
Resolutely to dismiss. But well-fried sheep
To keep and perchance sea bream: ah, there's the grub!

Love's Labor's Lost Act V Scene 2

When icicles hang by the wall,
And Dick the shepherd blows his nail,
And Tom bears logs into the hall,
And milk comes frozen home in pail,

When blood is nipped, and ways be foul,
Then nightly sings the staring owl,
To-whoo;
To-whit, to-whoo, a merry note,
While greasy Joan doth keel the pot.

When all aloud the wind doth blow,
And coughing drowns the parson's saw,
And birds sit brooding in the snow,
And Marian's nose looks red and raw,

When roasted crabs hiss in the bowl,
Then nightly sings the staring owl,
To-whoo;
To-whit, to-whoo, a merry note,
While greasy Joan doth keel the pot.

Dark Places

Where bicycles are chained to the wall
And Jack the Ripper eschewed jail
And Tom pays slags to take his call
Whose silk just covers bosom's tail

Where food is nicked, and ways be foul,
There nightly brings the glaring gowl,
To whom?
You, twit, you fool, a sorry goat;
Some sleazy crone doth reap the lot.

When well endowed the bints doth show
And knocking sounds through harlot's' door
And birds sit rooting for a beau
And Marian does rucks on beds of straw

When bloated lads kiss skinny molls
There nightly brings the glaring gowl,
To whom?
You, twit, you fool, a sorry goat;
Some sleazy crone doth steal the pot.

Hamlet Act 1, Scene 3

Yet here, Laertes! aboard, aboard, for shame!
The wind sits in the shoulder of your sail,
And you are stay'd for. There; my blessing with thee!
And these few precepts in thy memory
See thou character. Give thy thoughts no tongue,
Nor any unproportioned thought his act.
Be thou familiar, but by no means vulgar.
Those friends thou hast, and their adoption tried,
Grapple them to thy soul with hoops of steel;
But do not dull thy palm with entertainment
Of each new-hatch'd, unfledged comrade.

The Sponger

Get beer, Laertes! Reward! Deplore the game
Wherein sits the sober with no cocktail
Where none is paid for. There's no messing with me!
I see few regrets in thy treachery;
Be no predator! Drink what's bought no longer
Nor any free portion sought intact.
Be thou familiar, but by no means vulgar.
Those friends thou hast, extortion outrides.
Dapple their bowls with soups and ales;
But do not hold thy palm in containment
Of reach detached, your debts unpaid.

Twelfth Night Act II, Scene 5

*If this fall into thy hand, revolve. In my stars I am above thee;
but be not afraid of greatness: some are born great, some achieve
greatness, and some have greatness thrust upon them.*

*Thy Fates open their hands; let thy blood and spirit embrace
them; and to inure thyself to what thou art like to be, cast thy
humble slough, and appear fresh.*

*Be opposite with a kinsman, surly with servants; let thy tongue
tang arguments of state; put thyself into the trick of singularity.
She thus advises thee that sighs for thee.*

*Remember who commended thy yellow stockings, and wished to
see thee ever cross-gartered: I say, remember. Go to, thou art
made, if thou desirest to be so; if not, let me see thee a steward
still, the fellow of servants, and not worthy to touch Fortune's
fingers.*

Farewell. She that would alter services with thee.

Mentoring from the Darts Instructor

If it falls from thy hand, resolve. In darts, some land over twenty; but heed aught to play for straightness; some score bare eight, some esteem fame as handsome and gracious thrusts gain outcome.

Thy state controls thy hands; let fly good and will it encase zen as to endure by stealth to drop so artfully, lastly tumbling enough to steer success.

Be apposite with your game plan, surely and earnest; best among many far rumoured of late; fit thyself with the slickest angularity. Be thus advised: keep sights on glory.

Remember unattend thy fellows' mockings who wish to see thee lost, disordered. I pray, as mentor, so to mould thy game, if thou desirest to be so; if not, let me flee thee, a tutor still, but below a servant, not worthy to touch your fortune's fingers.

Then farewell; be that others walk to service with thee.

Richard III Act I, Scene I

Now is the winter of our discontent
Made glorious summer by this sun of York;
And all the clouds that lour'd upon our house
In the deep bosom of the ocean buried.
Now are our brows bound with victorious wreaths;
Our bruised arms hung up for monuments;
Our stern alarums changed to merry meetings,
Our dreadful marches to delightful measures.
Grim-visaged war hath smooth'd his wrinkled front;
And now, instead of mounting barded steeds
To fright the souls of fearful adversaries,
He capers nimbly in a lady's chamber
To the lascivious pleasing of a lute.

Winter Doldrums

How is it winter creates such discontent?
Late glorious summer, of no more sun to talk
And awesome clouds, rain pours and all does dowse
In some cheap, fulsome notion carried.
How can we rouse sound and luxuriance breathe?
When abuse harms, we're unsung of compliments.
Our ferned environs raged by heavy sheeting
Our nestled marshes now to blighted treasures;
Trimmed village flower beds bruised by wicked affront
And now, instead of routing barbed weeds
To incite the growth of cheerful plants and berries,
We shape the wintry daily labours
To the oblivious freezing of a brute.

Romeo and Juliet Act II, Scene 2

Juliet:
O Romeo, Romeo, wherefore art thou Romeo?
Deny thy father and refuse thy name;
Or if thou wilt not, be but sworn my love
And I'll no longer be a Capulet.

Romeo:
[Aside] Shall I hear more, or shall I speak at this?

Juliet:
'Tis but thy name that is my enemy:
Thou art thyself, though not a Montague.
What's Montague? It is nor hand nor foot,
Nor arm nor face, nor any other part
Belonging to a man. O be some other name!
What's in a name? That which we call a rose
By any other word would smell as sweet;
So Romeo would, were he not Romeo call'd,
Retain that dear perfection which he owes
Without that title. Romeo, doff thy name,
and for thy name, which is no part of thee,
Take all myself.

The Parting of Lovers

Juliet:
Home thee go, Romeo! E'ermore part now - home thee go!
To buy thy honour and excuse thy game?
For it now'd build nought, free to scorn my love
And I've no longing to capitulate.

Romeo:
Shall I plead more or shall I cease at this?

Juliet:
Mistrust and shame that give no clemency
Now guard myself, though not for want of you,
Lots of want for you. It is no grandeur put
Nor harm efface your heavy smothered heart
Or be daunting, if I can. O see some other aim!
What's to be gained? That which we held so close
In new discovered world just seems deplete;
So now understood, had not Romeo called,
And feigned sheer perfection to me bestowed
I'd out that trial. Romeo, drop off thy claim,
I'll make my claim to be no part of thee
And stay tall myself.

Othello Act V, Scene 2

Soft you, a word or two before you go
I have done the state some service and they know't.
No more of that, I pray you, in your letters,
When you shall these unlucky deeds relate,
Speak of me as I am. Nothing extenuate,
Nor set down aught in malice.

Wimbledon

Dropped two, a third to lose before you go.
I have won the sets with service and great strokes
But do come back, I'll play you, when you're better,
Then you can, please, plucky needs create.
Beat me if you can but nothing can extend your state
Though better fought with practice.

Macbeth, Act 5, Scene 5

To-morrow, and to-morrow, and to-morrow,
Creeps in this petty pace from day to day,
To the last syllable of recorded time;
And all our yesterdays have lighted fools
The way to dusty death. Out, out, brief candle!
Life's but a walking shadow, a poor player,
That struts and frets his hour upon the stage,
And then is heard no more. It is a tale
Told by an idiot, full of sound and fury,
Signifying nothing.

The Lost Gambler

To borrow, to borrow and more tomorrow,
Steeped in this debt disgrace always what may;
To the fast criminal, oh the sordid swine,
Hand all my better days as blighted fool.
From days of lusty stealth no doubt mishandled,
I'm just a balking cashflow, a poor payer,
That puts his bets empowered to pawn his wage
And then must earn some more. It is a tale
Told by an idiot, lost of pounds and glory,
Dignifying nothing.

Macbeth Act 2 Scene 1

Is this a dagger which I see before me,
The handle toward my hand? Come, let me clutch thee.
I have thee not, and yet I see thee still.
Art thou not, fatal vision, sensible
To feeling as to sight? or art thou but
A dagger of the mind, a false creation,
Proceeding from the heat-oppressed brain?
I see thee yet, in form as palpable
As this which now I draw.
Thou marshall'st me the way that I was going;
And such an instrument I was to use.
Mine eyes are made the fools o' the other senses,
Or else worth all the rest; I see thee still,
And on thy blade and dudgeon gouts of blood,
Which was not so before.

The Butler's Advice

Mistress, he staggers this sad creep before thee,
The vandal can hardly stand. Some, let me teach thee,
Bide chantry not, and better whisky swill.
Care thou not but make decision sensible
In keeping your birthright. So part now just,
No anger in the mind, no obligation,
Void pleading of complete distress and pain.
Pay heed thee yet this footman is incapable
And misery rich will store.
Thou harness't me to state what I saw showing;
In such, I implement against abuse,
Thy kindness made the tool of gross offences
I henceforth will arrest. I plead thee still,
As unafraid curmudgeon, vow to good
And show this sop the door.